FAMINE
THE WORLD REACTS

Th

Paul Bennett

Chrysalis Children's Books

FOREWORD

Disasters affect everyone. At some point in your life, you have a good chance of being caught in one or of knowing somebody who is caught in one.

For most of us, the disaster may be a car crash or a house fire, and the police, fire or ambulance service will be on hand to help. But for millions of people around the world, disasters happen far more often and are more catastrophic.

Some countries suffer frequent natural disasters, such as floods, earthquakes and droughts. They do not always have the resources to deal with the crisis and it is usually the poorest people who are the most affected and least able to recover.

War is a humanmade disaster that ruins people's lives. The effects of droughts and floods are made worse when there is war.

When people find they are unable to cope with a disaster, they need the help of aid agencies, such as the Red Cross.

Aid agencies react quickly to emergencies, bringing help to those in need. Usually it is when this international aid begins to flow that you hear about a disaster in the news.

The World Reacts series ties in closely with the work of the International Federation of Red Cross and Red Crescent Societies. The Federation coordinates international disaster relief and promotes development around the world, to prevent and alleviate human suffering. There is a Red Cross or Red Crescent society in almost every country of the world. Last year we helped 22 million people caught up in disaster.

This series will help you to understand the problems faced by people threatened by disaster and to see how you can help. We hope that you enjoy these books.

George Weber
Secretary General, International Federation
of Red Cross and Red Crescent Societies

◀ *The Red Cross symbol (left) was first created to protect the wounded in war and those who cared for them. The Red Crescent symbol (right) is used by Muslim countries around the world. Both symbols have equal status.*

CONTENTS

Words in **bold** appear in the glossary on page 31.

WHAT IS FAMINE?

Famine is a severe shortage of food. Large numbers of people do not get the food they need to stay fit and well. They become weak and may eventually die of starvation or disease.

Why do famines happen?

There are three main causes of famine: weather, war and poverty. Usually, two or more of these causes work together to create a famine.

Weather

Many people think that famines only happen in countries where **droughts** are common. When there is no rain for a long time, crops cannot grow and there is a shortage of food. But too much rain can also destroy harvests. Floods in North Korea in 1995 and 1996 left millions of people facing famine.

War

War turns farmers' fields into battlegrounds. Food cannot be grown and harvests are left to rot, as people leave their homes to escape the fighting.

Poverty

Poverty is another cause of famine. Plenty of food is grown around the world, but in many poor countries of the **South**, it is too expensive for people to buy, or it is grown only for **export** and not for those who need it.

▲ *For many people in the South, a good harvest depends on rainfall. Without water, crops shrivel and die in the hot sun.*

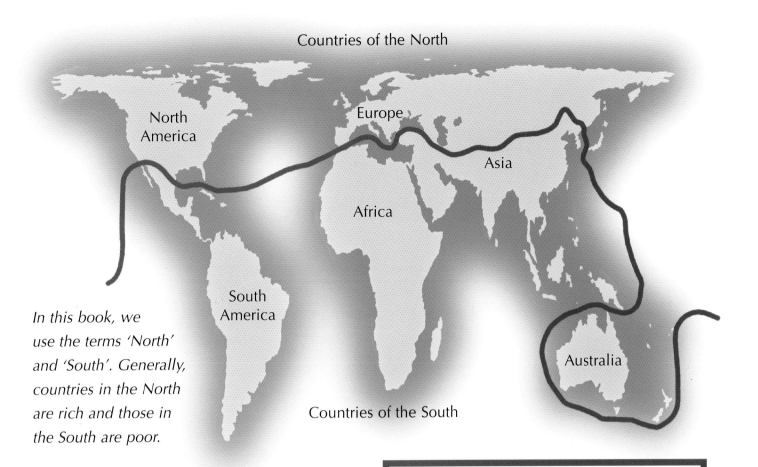

Countries of the North

North America

Europe

Asia

Africa

South America

Australia

Countries of the South

In this book, we use the terms 'North' and 'South'. Generally, countries in the North are rich and those in the South are poor.

Famine myths

What do you know about famine? Here are a few famine myths to think about:

● 'Famine only happens in the countries of the South.' In the past there have been famines all over the world, for example in Ireland in 1845, Russia in the 1930s and Greece after the Second World War.

● 'People who face famine do nothing to help themselves.' People who live in areas where food shortages are common are very skilled at getting the best out of the land. They do not sit and wait for help to arrive from the **North**.

● 'Nothing is done to tackle the causes of famine.' As you will see from reading this book, people all over the world are fighting the causes of food shortages.

The world maps used in this book are Peters' projection maps. Peters' projection – named after Arno Peters who made the map – is an accurate way of seeing the world, because it shows the actual size of countries.

Aid in action

Famine: The World Reacts looks at what happens during a famine and how the world can help. It takes real-life examples of food shortages and famines from around the world and looks at the help given by governments and **aid agencies**.

The book aims to help you understand the problems of those who face famine and hunger year after year and to see what can be done to help.

FLIGHT FROM THE LAND

In many of the countries of the South, people grow their own food on small plots of land. When crops are good, families have enough food to last until the next harvest.

Threatened by famine

In areas where droughts are common, people are very skilled at getting the best out of the land.

When their harvests are good, they store extra food and seed for the future. But if the next harvest fails, these stores soon run out.

When this happens, there is the danger of famine.

When food becomes scarce, people may travel to the towns to look for work. If they are unable to find jobs and send money home, they are forced to sell everything they own – tools, animals and even their land – to buy food. When there is nothing left to sell, whole families are forced to leave their homes in search of food.

◀ *These men are leaving their homes in Ethiopia to escape the effects of drought and famine.*

Hunger in the towns

A failing harvest is a common reason for people to leave home to look for food. But the victims of famine and food shortages are not just those who live on the land. People who live in towns and cities feel the effects of food shortages as much as those who live in the countryside.

This is especially so in cities where there is extreme poverty, such as the **shanty towns** of Rio de Janeiro in Brazil (above). When food is in short supply, the price of food rises. This means that people have to pay more for less food. Often they simply cannot afford to buy food and may face starvation.

Sudan 1991
People on the move

Sudan suffered droughts in both 1990 and 1991, resulting in serious food shortages. The threat of famine was made worse by **civil war** in the south of the country.

Three-quarters of Sudan's population depend on farming for their living, so millions of people left their homes to head for towns and cities in search of food.

Ethiopian **refugees** were also on the move. They fled into Sudan to escape drought, famine and fighting in their own country.

Help at hand

The Sudanese **Red Crescent** set up feeding centres throughout the country to provide people with much-needed food supplies.

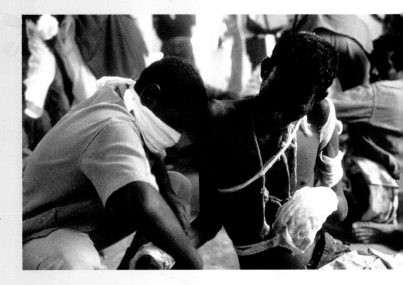

▲ *Many of the Ethiopian refugees who arrived in Sudan were soldiers in need of medical help. This soldier is having his wounds bandaged by a Red Cross medical worker.*

In the Red Sea Hills area of the country, these feeding centres gave out food five times a day to the children who were suffering the most.

An Austrian **Red Cross** worker in one of the feeding centres, Uschi Schöll, tells the story of a five-year-old boy called Mohamed Tahir:

'When he first came to the feeding centre, he was **malnourished**... He came all by himself, always on time. Because he came so regularly, he quickly put on weight and became well again.'

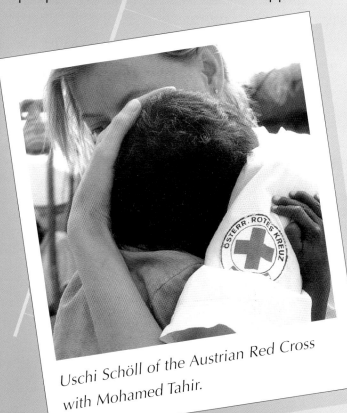

Uschi Schöll of the Austrian Red Cross with Mohamed Tahir.

RELIEF CAMPS

A relief camp is a place set up by aid workers to care for people escaping famine or another kind of disaster.

Arriving at the camps

People who have left their homes in search of food and water arrive exhausted at relief camps. Those who have come from more remote areas may have walked hundreds of kilometres to get help at the camps.

In some areas, aid workers have a store of food already in place. They set up feeding stations and stoves for cooking and arrange toilets and supplies of water for people arriving at the camps. They do their best to help those most in need, but the numbers at the camps rise by the day, as more people flee their homes in search of food.

▼ *This is the Korem relief camp which was set up to provide help for victims of the 1984 famine in Ethiopia.*

Going hungry

Every night 500 million children go to bed hungry. And every day they wake up to face another day without a good meal.

There are more poorly-fed children in the world today than ever before. People who do not receive enough food or the right food are said to be malnourished. This means that they do not have a balanced diet to keep their bodies fit and strong.

Malnourished children grow more slowly than well-fed children and may have **deformities**. The boy in the photo above is malnourished.

Kenya 1992

The Liboi relief camp

Liboi in eastern Kenya is near the border with Somalia. A relief camp was set up there for refugees from Somalia who were fleeing the effects of drought and war in their own country.

The road to the Liboi camp was littered with the bones of animals, as crops and farm animals had been destroyed by the drought that plagued the land.

People arrived at the camp, tired and hungry. Some had walked over 200 kilometres beneath the burning sun. The more seriously ill people were sent to a hospital in the camp where they received medical care.

◄ *Somalian refugees carry firewood for cooking at the Liboi relief camp. This camp may be their home for many months or even years.*

An aid worker described the emergency situation at the Liboi camp:

❝ The French doctors no longer have time to sleep… The number of adults and children suffering from malnutrition is enormous and in no way matches the number of health workers. If people are to be saved, there must be more doctors, more time, more money.❞

► *A small boy is treated at one of the camp's medical centres.*

EMERGENCY RESPONSE

As famine conditions become worse, more people arrive at relief camps in search of food and emergency food supplies begin to run out.

Helping the hungry

When news of a famine reaches the rest of the world, aid agencies move quickly to organize relief.

Emergency managers from the agencies are sent into famine areas to see what help is needed. **Aid** in the form of food, tents, blankets and medical supplies is sent to the camps. Thousands of people need shelter and something to keep them warm if they are to survive. They also need medical help to prevent the spread of disease. People who are weak with hunger are in danger of catching diseases in crowded camps, where conditions are sometimes dirty and unhygienic.

Governments around the world may also help – by sending aid themselves or by donating money to agencies.

▼ *The World Food Program (WFP), part of the **United Nations (UN)**, drops parcels of food to more remote areas struck by hunger and famine.*

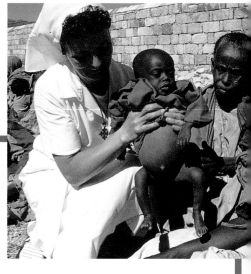

Children at risk

Children are often the most affected by famine. They become tired and weak with hunger and this makes them more likely to become ill. Crowded camps allow diseases to spread quickly, threatening the lives of many children.

Doctors and nurses are sent into famine areas to prevent the spread of disease. One aid agency, **Médecins Sans Frontières (MSF)**, provides basic health care and works to improve conditions in the camps. It also runs vaccination programmes, giving people injections to stop them catching diseases.

Bangladesh 1995
Flood and famine

Famine is not only caused by drought and bad harvests, it can also be caused by natural disasters such as floods. Bangladesh is a small country in Asia that has suffered famine and food shortages because of serious floods. Storms called cyclones flood the land, destroy crops and leave survivors with no food or shelter.

In 1995, a cyclone hit Bangladesh. Nine-year-old Mohammed Ibrahim tells his story:

'It had been raining heavily for three or four days. On the last day, the water started to come into the house. My brother and I drove the cattle to the shelter... I was trembling with fear. We stayed in the shelter all night while the floods swept away the land... My house was destroyed, but we were safe.'

Nine-year-old Mohammed Ibrahim, shown second from left, survived the 1995 cyclone in Bangladesh.

Bangladesh suffers from floods year after year. This means that aid agencies can plan ahead to prevent famine. After the cyclone, there was damage to crops and water supplies. But aid agencies, such as ACTIONAID, were able to respond quickly, providing people with shelter, new seeds for planting and clean water.

◄ *These people are being driven from their homes by rising flood waters in Bangladesh.*

DELIVERING AID

Aid is mostly sent by ship to famine-stricken countries. Relief supplies are unloaded at the ports ready to be sent out to the camps by truck.

Getting the aid through

While the ships are on their way, governments and aid agencies work together to prepare for their arrival. If the roads are good, aid can be transported quickly. Dirt-track roads in more remote areas may slow things down.

During a civil war, aid workers may have to work with both sides in the conflict to get supplies through. In these conditions, it may take days for aid to reach the camps.

Aid is sometimes flown into more remote areas. But the amount of aid that can be carried by plane is small compared to the amount that a convoy of trucks can carry. A **Hercules** plane can deliver up to 20 tonnes of relief supplies in one flight, while a large truck convoy can transport 2000 tonnes. Many flights may be necessary.

Delivering clean water

A clean water supply to relief camps is essential. Without clean water, people are in danger of catching life-threatening diseases which are carried in dirty water.

So as soon as possible, aid agencies work out how to deliver clean water to camps. They treat available supplies of water to kill the germs that cause disease or they drill bore holes in the ground, so that water can be brought to the surface and stored in large tanks.

When there are no water sources nearby, water will be delivered to the camps in huge water tankers.

▼ *A convoy of Red Cross trucks carries food aid across barren land in Ethiopia.*

Zaire 1994
Crisis in Goma

In 1994, more than one million Rwandans crossed the border into Goma in Zaire (now called the Democratic Republic of Congo) in just four days. They left Rwanda to escape fighting between rival groups.

This was the fastest movement of refugees ever recorded and it took aid agencies by surprise. Ten thousand people were crossing the border between Rwanda and Zaire every hour. Many were dying of **dehydration** and disease. Clean water supplies were essential.

An aid worker described how agencies worked together to help:

'Médecins Sans Frontières staff set up clinics in the middle of all the chaos and worked day and night for days on end. OXFAM staff set up water tanks which saved thousands of lives.'

▲ *Rwandans stream across the border into Zaire in 1994.*

▼ *Huge tanks were set up in Goma to provide clean water.*

Trucks were urgently needed to deliver aid to the camps being set up in Goma. But because everyone had been taken by surprise, this took some time.

Airlifts were the only way to deliver aid immediately. Forty flights a day from around the world brought relief supplies into the small Goma airfield. For weeks and weeks, the planes never stopped coming.

WHEN AID ARRIVES

After the trucks are unloaded at the camps, they travel back to the port to pick up more supplies. There will be many deliveries during an emergency.

Feeding stations

Feeding stations are set up in relief camps to distribute food. It is difficult to give out food to tens of thousands of people every day. At the beginning of a crisis, food is unloaded from trucks and shared out. Extra food is given to children and adults suffering from malnutrition.

As deliveries continue, a **reserve** stock of food is stored in huge tents. People are given a **ration** of food that will last them a few days. They are also given pots and pans to cook with. Food is often given to the women to cook for their families.

Plastic sheeting and poles are delivered so that shelters can be built. Clothing and blankets are given out to make people more comfortable and doctors at the health centres receive medical supplies.

▼ *These boys are preparing their own food at a feeding station in Sudan.*

Returning home

Governments often want people in relief camps to return home as soon as possible. But to return home without any help will not solve their problems. They have no money to buy seed to grow crops and many will have sold their farm tools. This is why it is important that governments and aid agencies give people what they need to start again.

For example, Somalian refugees (above) were given **hoes** by aid agencies, so that they could return home to their villages and start growing crops again. If people return home too late to plant their seeds, they need food to last until the next harvest.

Iraq 1991
Helping Kurdish refugees

The Kurds are people who have lived in Northern Iraq for thousands of years. Many of them would like an **independent** Kurdistan, as they are not allowed to keep their own language and customs in Iraq. In 1991, the Kurds rebelled against the Iraqi leader, Saddam Hussein, and his forces. This rebellion was unsuccessful, and one and a half million Kurds had to leave their homes for the Turkish–Iraqi border to escape Iraqi attacks. The Iraqi government would not allow aid supplies to be delivered to the Kurds who were on the move in northern Iraq.

▲ *The Red Crescent Society delivered tents to Kurds stranded near the Turkish–Iraqi border.*

▼ *The Kurds were so hungry that soldiers were forced to fire in to the air to prevent a rush after a food delivery.*

Aid against the odds

Near the border, tens of thousands of people became stranded on a freezing mountain range in urgent need of food, water, fuel and medicine. Up to 5000 children a month were dying of malnutrition. The United Nations was forced to set up **safe zones** without agreement from Iraq to get aid through.

Through all the difficulties, aid agencies continued to supply emergency relief to Kurdish camps and are now working on long-term ways of helping the Kurds.

RELIEF GROUPS

A famine can involve up to 200 different groups all working to help those most in need. Famine relief takes much organization and money to carry out.

Aid agencies

Aid agencies, such as the Red Cross and Red Crescent, Médecins Sans Frontières, Save the Children Fund and ACTIONAID, help famine victims all over the world. Many are charities that rely on donations of money to carry out their work.

Governments all over the world also help when there is an emergency. They do this in many different ways – they give money to aid agencies or they send food, tents and blankets themselves.

The United Nations (UN) gets involved too. The World Food Program is the UN's food aid organization, and helps countries affected by famine and food shortages.

Volunteers – people who offer to work for no pay – are sent to famine areas.

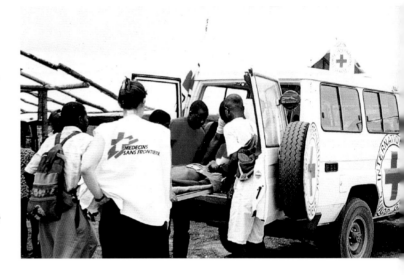

▲ *The Red Cross and Médecins Sans Frontières working together to help people in Liberia.*

Volunteers include doctors and nurses who give medical help, and engineers who set up toilets and water supplies in relief camps.

Working together

There needs to be cooperation between relief groups involved in a famine. This prevents delays in getting aid through to the camps, which would otherwise result in more suffering.

A **Code of Conduct** has been developed by a group of aid agencies to encourage everyone to work together. One of the recommendations, for example, is that governments allow aid to enter freely into their country, so that it can be sent to relief camps without unnecessary hold-ups.

Southern Africa 1992
International relief effort

In the early 1990s, there was a long drought in eleven countries in southern Africa. For the first time this century, none of the countries in the region had grain to export to their neighbours, and huge quantities of food had to be brought into Southern Africa. Only help from countries all over the world could prevent famine for 18 million African people.

Emergency food

Food supplies usually bought locally by the World Food Program (WFP) and other aid agencies were no longer available because of the drought. The WFP appealed for 1 700 000 tonnes of emergency food. The response to the appeal was good. The **European Union** and the United States, for example, sent 225 000 tonnes of maize to famine victims in Mozambique, one of the countries that was worst hit by the drought in Southern Africa.

Most of the food was given out through feeding programmes already set up by the World Food Program, aid agencies and the governments of the region. Food was distributed on a scale never before tried in southern Africa.

▲ The maize crop failed in Zimbabwe in 1992 because of the drought that struck the region.

◀ These villagers are carrying food rations home from a food distribution centre in Mozambique.

FUNDRAISING

Most of us have seen pictures of starving children on television. They appeal to our feelings and make us want to give money to those suffering because of famine.

Appeals for aid

When famine strikes, aid agencies make special appeals to raise money with advertisements in newspapers and poster campaigns.

Fundraising is an important part of the work of aid agencies all year round. Fundraising events, such as sponsored runs, are fun ways ordinary people can help. The money raised helps people in an emergency, but it is also used to help people help themselves. Aid agencies run long-term projects to enable people to grow their own food and to train them with the skills they need. This is a very important part of their work.

▼ *People do sponsored stunts, such as parachuting, to raise money for charity.*

Where the money goes

Every year, hundreds of millions of pounds are raised by charities from donations from the public and from national governments. But where does this money go?

About four per cent of the money goes on running costs, information and education services. Eight per cent goes on fundraising and publicity. And 88 per cent is spent on ways of improving people's lives all around the world. This work includes providing food, clean drinking water (above) and shelter, and improving transport and roads, health services and ways of producing crops.

Ethiopia 1984

Attracting attention

Pictures of starving people are a powerful way of drawing our attention to famine. In 1984, the world was shocked by the famine in Ethiopia. The Ethiopian crop failed in 1983, but governments did nothing until the horrific effects of the famine were shown on television.

The power of television

On 23 October 1984, the BBC showed a seven-minute film of the starving people in the Korem relief camp in Ethiopia (see page 8). Through television, newspapers and magazines, the world soon became aware of the scale of the suffering of famine victims in Ethiopia and governments began to help. This example clearly shows the power of television to attract the world's attention to famine and to change events.

Live Aid

During the Ethiopian famine, Live Aid was started by the British pop singer, Bob Geldof. Through the sale of records and pop concerts in London and Philadelphia in the USA, people all over the world gave tens of millions of pounds for famine relief in Africa.

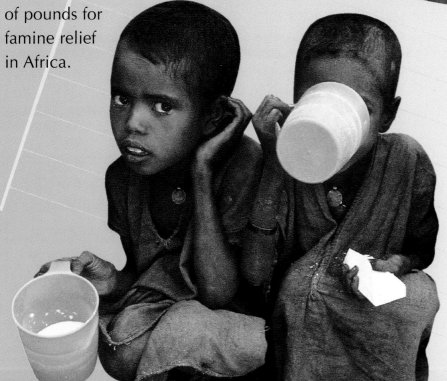

▲ This Live Aid concert was held in London in 1985 to raise money for famine relief.

CREEPING DISASTER

Disasters such as earthquakes and floods are sudden and dramatic. But famines are slower to happen and it is not always clear when aid agencies should act.

Preventing disaster

Short-term shortages of food are common in many parts of the world, so it is not always easy for aid agencies to predict when a famine is likely to happen.

Aid agency workers have a good understanding of conditions and problems in many countries of the world. They can often give warnings about emergencies that are about to happen. A quick reaction from aid agencies can save many lives.

Aid workers carry out checks on harvests and food prices in areas where food shortages are common. For example, in 1994 and 1995, when the rains failed in Ethiopia and food prices rose, aid agencies sent food to the villages most at risk, so that people could stay on their land.

▲ *An aid worker checks harvests in Angola and offers advice to farmers.*

Warning signs

When food becomes scarce, people start to change the way they do things to survive. Aid workers notice these changes and so build up a picture of what is happening locally. For example, people start moving from the country to find work in the towns, and they sell their animals, clothes and farm tools to raise money for food. They start to eat 'famine' food, such as leaves and bark. The boys in the photo are eating seeds from waterlilies to survive.

Italy 1998

A global warning system

The United Nations' Food and Agriculture Organization in Rome, Italy, has a system which warns aid agencies about possible harvest failure and famine.

This system is called the Global Information and Early Warning System (GIEWS) and is an important tool in the fight against famine and hunger.

Prediction and prevention

GIEWS tries to predict famine in several ways. It follows the buying and selling of basic foods around the world and gives warnings of food shortages and food **surpluses**. It also monitors the weather, **pests**, such as **locusts**, and animal and plant diseases, because these are all things that affect the supply of food.

▲ *These boys are trying to fight a swarm of locusts in Mauritania in northern Africa.*

Satellites at work

Satellites orbiting the Earth are also used as part of the system. Weather satellites monitor rainfall and cloud cover and produce a detailed picture of weather conditions all over the world.

Survey satellites take pictures of huge areas of land. From the photos, it is possible to see how much land is used for crop growing, how much food is produced, the best areas for growing crops and how to get water to these areas.

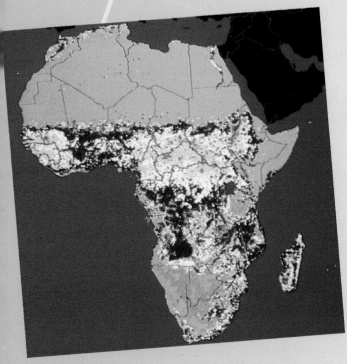

◄ *This satellite photo shows areas of Africa that have been turned to desert (see yellow areas), partly because land has been overused.*

FOOD AND POVERTY

Poverty is one of the main causes of famine. Rich people do not really suffer when there are food shortages. They can buy the food they need even when prices rise.

Food security

Poor people do not have 'food security'. Food security means that all people in a country – both rich and poor – can buy food that is good for them and in the amounts they need to lead an active, healthy life. A good way of giving people more food security is to encourage them to grow and harvest more crops and to use farming methods that make the best use of a family's resources.

People can be trained to control animal diseases which destroy whole herds. Small loans of money will help farmers to buy a few animals, or **pesticides** to protect their crops. This training and support gives people more food security and improves their lives. They have more food to eat and more to sell. Projects to help people help themselves are an important part of the work of aid agencies.

▲ *This farmer in India is spraying his crops with pesticides to protect his harvest.*

Development schemes

Aid can also be used to fight the causes of poverty and for long-term **development** projects. 'Food for work' and 'cash for work' schemes have been used with some success. Workers are paid with food (food for work) or money (cash for work) to improve conditions in their local area. Schemes include projects to prevent **soil erosion** by planting trees (left) or projects to build wells, schools and hospitals.

Peru 1990s

The Cusco project

The ancient Inca capital of Cusco lies 3200 metres up in the Andes mountains of Peru. The area in and around Cusco is one of the poorest parts of Peru, and food insecurity has made it difficult for villagers to support themselves and their families. In 1985, Save the Children Fund (SCF) started working in the small town of El Descanso. The aim was to help villagers raise their standard of living by improving farming methods. In 1987, SCF handed over the project to a Peruvian aid agency called KAUSAY.

▼ These sheep have been treated with chemicals to protect them from insects that can harm their health.

Improving people's lives

The KAUSAY project has encouraged farmers to plan ahead how many seeds they plant and when. This has helped to protect the community from the effects of drought.

Irrigation projects have increased the supply of water to farmland and tree planting has helped to prevent soil erosion. Animals have been protected against **parasites**, improving the health of the herds.

KAUSAY has passed on the views of local people to the government of Peru. This has resulted in the government setting up its own programmes in and around Cusco.

◄ Irrigation ditches have increased the supply of water to farmland.

MONEY MATTERS

In the 1970s and 1980s, poor countries in Africa and Latin America borrowed money from governments of the North. But for many countries, these loans have led to great hardship.

Foreign debts

Money borrowed from foreign governments and banks must be paid back within a certain period of time and with an extra amount, called interest, paid on top. Many countries of the South could not pay the interest, and had to borrow more money.

These countries were forced to sell their goods abroad to pay back loans. Farmers were encouraged to grow **cash crops**, such as coffee, to sell abroad, so even less land was available to grow food for local people.

Sometimes borrowed money was not spent wisely. It was spent on weapons for war, instead of health and education.

War and natural disasters added to these problems, leading to hunger and famine.

◄ *This girl is picking coffee – one of the main cash crops produced for export in Zambia.*

War and famine

There is a strong link between civil war and famine. Farmers who are caught up in armed conflict cannot plant their seeds or harvest their crops. Those who keep sheep and cattle find it difficult to feed and look after their animals. When markets close, they cannot sell their animals to raise money for food. People leave their villages in search of safety and food. This puts great pressure on the people living in the towns who may be short of food themselves.

Mozambique 1990s

Money for arms

Mozambique gained independence from its Portuguese rulers in 1975. But in the years that followed, the country faced problems because of civil war, drought and government decisions that damaged its **economy**.

From 1987, with support from international banking organizations, Mozambique was encouraged to change its economic policies, but it had to borrow money from abroad to do this. Mozambique spent much of this money on arms, which it bought from Western **arms dealers** and governments.

◀ *The government bought weapons for war instead of spending borrowed money on ordinary people.*

A lasting peace?

A peace agreement was signed in October 1992 which ended the conflict in Mozambique, and **elections** followed in 1994. Peace meant that the country could rebuild its economy rather than spending money on guns and bullets.

Now that there is peace, international banks plan to reduce the amount of money owed by Mozambique. This will not happen for several years and, until it does, Mozambique will continue to be one of the poorest countries in the world.

▶ *Peace should mean that more money can be spent on children's education.*

LAND AND POWER

Poverty in many countries of the South has meant that people must sell their crops abroad. They often have to give up their best land to grow crops for the countries of the North instead of for themselves.

Cash crops

Crops which are grown to sell to the richer nations of the world are called cash crops. Cash crops include coffee, cocoa and bananas. Many countries have become dependent on one cash crop for money.

Lots of money has been spent on large farms and **plantations** to grow these crops. The workers on these farms usually work part-time and are often badly paid. The people who grow cash crops often receive low prices for what they produce. Huge profits are made by the companies who buy the crops, and then process and package them elsewhere in the world.

▲ *Workers in a coffee plantation in Ethiopia.*

The colonial legacy

Many of the poorest countries of the world were once ruled by European countries. Britain, France and the Netherlands ruled large parts of Africa and Asia. Portugal and Spain ruled much of Latin America and the Caribbean. These European countries set up sugar, tea and cotton plantations to export these crops abroad to earn money.

Most of the **colonized** countries now rule themselves, but often the best land is still in the hands of a few plantation owners. This unequal distribution of land is one of the reasons for poverty in many of the former **colonies**.

Malawi 1990s

Food shortages – a way of life

Eight out of ten people in Malawi work on the land. But most of the land is owned by people who grow tobacco for export. Tobacco is Malawi's main cash crop and brings in three-quarters of the money it earns from exports. Tobacco, tea and sugar are grown on large, modern farms using land that used to provide a living for local people. But local people can no longer farm this land. They have become poorer and poorer as a result, and food shortages have become a way of life for them.

◀ *Tobacco workers in Malawi. Tobacco is Malawi's main cash crop for export abroad.*

▼ *Jane, age nine, stands in front of her family's maize field in the north of Malawi.*

Improving lives in Malawi

Problems of poverty and food insecurity have been made worse by price increases in Malawi's main food crop, maize, and fertilizers for protecting crops. The effect of a drought in the country could be disastrous. This is why it is so important that aid agencies give help to small farmers to develop their land. Aid on a local level is the only way to give people the power to grow their own food and the chance to lead more secure lives.

FOOD FOR THOUGHT

Famines do not happen because some countries are worse than others at growing food. Famines have happened in places with some of the best soil and growing conditions in the world.

Feeding the planet

One of the biggest famine myths is that people starve because there are too many mouths to feed. In fact, there is more than enough food grown around the world to feed everyone. We do not need to produce any more food, we just need to share it out more fairly.

For example, there are countries in the North that have huge surpluses of food, called **food mountains**. This food is often wasted, while others in the world go hungry.

Emergency food aid is sometimes needed to save lives. But it does not solve the root causes of food insecurity.

An important way of preventing hunger and famine is for poorer countries to improve their economies and their people's incomes. Then governments would have the extra money to buy food from abroad if there were shortages. With a reliable supply of food, prices would stay low and ordinary people would not go hungry.

Long-term projects

Emergency food aid is a short-term and expensive way of responding to a crisis. It does not deal with the problems which cause famine. This is why aid agencies encourage people to start up and run their own projects. They train them with the skills they need, so they can help themselves.

This does not happen overnight. Supplying seeds and tools is quick and easy, but improving the local economy takes time. But this is what must happen if food insecurity is to be removed from millions of people's lives.

◄ *This wheat mountain in the United States will be wasted when others in the world go hungry.*

Bolivia 1990s
The Calcha project

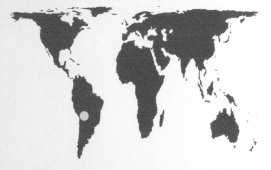

Calcha is an area in the mountains of Bolivia. Most of its 6500 people live in poverty and have a poor diet. Most of the land is unsuitable for growing crops and so for five months of the year, men and women are forced to leave their homes to find work on large farms and in industry in the east of Bolivia and in Argentina. But through projects run by a Bolivian aid agency and supported by ACTIONAID, local people are working to make themselves independent and to improve the quality of their lives.

For example, in the village of Yuraj Cancha, people are planting a greater variety of fruit trees. The fruit is sold to provide income for families and some of it is processed to sell as jam. People also produce honey from their bees and cheese from their goats' milk to sell.

▶ *Concrete irrigation canals have been built to water crops, such as maize, potatoes and beans.*

Lucia Mora de Gira (left) weaving with one of the other women on the project.

The women of Calcha have learnt to weave as part of a successful textiles project. They sell their cloth at local markets and further afield.

Lucia Mora de Gira has been working with the textiles project for six years:

❛I've seen great changes in that time. The women have got used to saying what they want. Because they earn money for their families, they have become much more confident.❜

HOW YOU CAN HELP

Food gives us energy to work and play, and helps us to stay fit and healthy. There is enough food to feed the world, but too many people go hungry.

● Look at the labels on the food you buy at the supermarket. How many items are grown in the countries of the South? Make a world map to show where the foods come from.

● Have another look at the famine myths on page 5. Compare your ideas about famine before reading this book to what you know now.

● Collect newspaper reports on famine. What are the reasons given for the famine?

● Find out about aid agencies you would like to help (see addresses below). With your friends, collect unwanted clothes, books and toys and donate them to your chosen charity.

● Choose an aid agency you would like to raise money for. Organize a fundraising activity, such as a sponsored run or swim. Design your own sponsorship form and give information about how the money will be spent.

Finding out more

Write to aid agencies or visit their web sites to find out about their work and how you can help.

British Red Cross
9 Grosvenor Crescent
London SW1X 7EJ
Telephone: 0171 235 5454
http://www.redcross.org.uk

OXFAM
274 Banbury Road
Oxford OX2 7DZ
Telephone: 01865 313600
http://www.oxfam.org.uk

Save the Children Fund (SCF)
17 Grove Lane
London SE5 8RD
Telephone: 0171 703 5400
http://www.oneworld.org/scf/

ACTIONAID
Hamlyn House
Macdonald Road
Archway
London N19 5PG
Telephone: 0171 281 4101
http://www.oneworld.org/actionaid

Médecins Sans Frontières (MSF)
124–132 Clerkenwell Road
London EC1R 5DL
Telephone: 0171 713 5600
http://www.msf.org

United Nations Children's
Fund (UNICEF)
55 Lincolns Inn Fields
London WC2A 3NB
Telephone: 0171 405 5592
http://www.unicef.org.uk

United Nations High Commissioner
for Refugees (UNHCR)
Millbank Tower
21–24 Millbank
London
SW1P 4QP
Telephone: 0171 828 9191
http://www.unhcr.ch

The International Federation of Red
Cross and Red Crescent Societies
17 chemin des Crêts
Petit-Saconnex
PO Box 372
CH-1211
Geneva 19
Switzerland
Telephone: 00 41 22 730 4222
http://www.ifrc.org

GLOSSARY

aid Resources given by one country, or organization, to another country. Aid is given to help people in an emergency and to improve their lives in the longer term.

aid agency An organization that helps people when there is a disaster and runs long-term projects to help people in poorer countries.

arms dealer Someone who makes a profit from selling weapons, such as guns, tanks and rockets.

cash crop A crop that is grown for sale rather than for use by the farmer. Examples are coffee, tea and bananas.

civil war A war between sides *within* a country.

Code of Conduct Guidelines for people to follow when there is a crisis.

colonized This describes countries that were settled and governed by other countries.

colony A country ruled by another nation.

deformity A part of the body that is badly shaped because it did not grow properly.

dehydration Lack of water in the body.

development The use of resources in a country to increase the standard of living of its people.

drought A long period of time without rainfall.

economy The activities of a country which help it to earn money.

election A vote to decide the government of a country.

emergency manager Someone who is an expert in assessing people's needs in a crisis.

European Union A group of European countries who work together.

export To sell or move products to another country.

food mountain A store of surplus food. Food mountains include grain, beef and butter mountains.

Hercules A type of large plane designed for transporting heavy loads.

hoe A tool used by a farmer to turn the soil.

independent Free from rule by another country.

irrigation Supplying land with water along canals or ditches to improve crop growth.

locust An insect that swarms and eats through fields of crops.

malnourished A malnourished person is weak and thin through lack of food or not eating the right kinds of food.

Médecins Sans Frontières (MSF) An aid agency which offers medical help in a crisis. The name is French for 'doctors without borders'.

North Wealthier countries, mainly in the northern part of the world. Although they are further south on a world map, Australia and New Zealand are also included in the countries of the North. See map on page 5.

parasite A tiny insect that lives on animals and causes disease.

pest A creature, such as a locust, that damages crops.

pesticide A chemical used by farmers to kill pests.

plantation A farm that grows cash crops on a huge scale.

ration A measured amount of food. Food has to be rationed in times of crisis, for example during a famine or war.

Red Crescent A Muslim aid agency that is part of the Red Cross movement. Its symbol is a red crescent.

Red Cross An international aid agency which was set up in 1863. Its symbol is a red cross.

refugee Someone who has fled to another country because their life or freedom is in danger.

reserve A stock of food set aside for future use.

safe zone A protected area where refugees can live until it is safe to return home.

shanty town A part of a town or city where people live in very poor conditions.

soil erosion The wearing away of soil by rain or wind.

South Poor countries, mainly in the southern part of the world. See map on page 5.

surplus An amount of food that is left over after what is needed has been eaten.

United Nations (UN) An organization of countries around the world which encourages world peace and offers help to people in a crisis.

31

INDEX

First published in Great Britain in 1999 by

Chrysalis Children's Books
An imprint of Chrysalis Books Group plc
The Chrysalis Building, Bramley Road,
London W10 6SP

Copyright in this format © Chrysalis Books Group plc 1999
Text copyright © Paul Bennet 1999

Paperback edition published in 2003

Series editor Julie Hill
Series designer Simeen Karim
Consultants Dr Peter Walker and Elizabeth Bassant
Picture researcher Diana Morris

ISBN 1 85561 792 7 (hb)
ISBN 1 84138 951 X (pb)

British Library Cataloguing in Publication Data for this book is available from the British Library.

Printed in Hong Kong

Photographic credits

ACTIONAID /Steve Morgan: 29t, 29b /Liba Taylor: 11t. Alfred/Sipa/Rex Features: 15b. Mohamed Amin/Camera Press: 10t. Jean-Louis Atalan/Sygma: back cover. Trygve Bølstad/Panos Pictures: 9b, 20t, 27t. British Red Cross/Barbara Geary: 7b. Charles Caratini/Sygma: 13b. Daniel Dancer/Still Pictures: 28. DRA/Still Pictures: 21b. Mark Edwards/Still Pictures: 6t, 22b. FAO Photo: 21t. Frilet/Sipa/Rex Features: front cover, 3, 19b. Ron Giling/Still Pictures: 26t. T. Haley/Sipa/Rex Features: 13t. Chip Hires/Gamma/Frank Spooner Pictures: 11b. Jim Holmes/ Panos Pictures: 22t. D. Hudson/Sygma: title page & 6b. ICRC: 2, 14b, 16 /T. Bertelsen: 7t. Peter Lamberti/Getty Images: 18b. Guy Mansfield/Panos Pictures: 25t. MSF/Remco Bohle: 30. Bruce Paton/Panos Pictures: 25b. Heine Pedersen/Still Pictures: 12. Rex Features: 15t, 19t. Carlos Reyes-Manzo/Andes Press Agency: 14t. SCF/Sylvia Beales: 23t /Mike Wells: 8b. Chris Steele-Perkins/ Magnum Photos: 20b. Simon Townsley/ Camera Press: 18t. UNHCR/P. Moumteis: 8t /B. Press: 9t. UNICEF/C. Andrews: 27b/Fran Antmann: 23b /Isaac: 25b/ Lemoyne: 4. WFP/Alex Joe: 10b /Mercedes Sayagues: 17b. Greg Williams/Rex Features: 17t.

With thanks to the following for case study material:
ACTIONAID pp 11 & 29; British Red Cross p7; Save the Children Fund p23; and UNHCR pp 9, 13 & 17.